DATE			

Bhopal

GREAT DISASTERS
REFORMS and RAMIFICATIONS

Bhopal

John Riddle

CHELSEA HOUSE PUBLISHERS
Philadelphia

Frontispiece: India, the second most populous country in the world, is located in south central Asia. Over one billion people reside on the Indian subcontinent.

CHELSEA HOUSE PUBLISHERS

Editor in Chief Sally Cheney
Director of Production Kim Shinners
Creative Manager Takeshi Takahashi
Manufacturing Manager Diann Grasse

Staff for BHOPAL

Assistant Editor Susan Naab
Picture Researcher Sarah Bloom
Production Assistant Jaimie Winkler
Series Designer Takeshi Takahashi
Cover Designer Keith Trego
Layout 21st Century Publishing and Communications, Inc.

First Printing

1 3 5 7 9 8 6 4 2

The Chelsea House World Wide Web address is
http://www.chelseahouse.com

Library of Congress Cataloging-in-Publication Data

Riddle, John.
    Bhopal : great disasters, reforms and ramifications / John Riddle.
        p. cm.
Summary: Presents an account of the 1984 chemical accident at the Union Carbide plant in Bhopal, India, and explores how the investigation of such accidents can lead to safety reform.
Includes bibliographical references and index.
    ISBN 0-7910-6741-6 (hardcover)
    1. Bhopal Union Carbide Plant Disaster, Bhopal, India, 1984—Juvenile literature. 2. Pesticide industry—Accidents—India—Bhopal—Juvenile literature. 3. Chemical industry—Accidents—India—Bhopal—Juvenile literature. 4. Methyl isocyanate—Toxicology—India—Bhopal—Juvenile literature. [1. Bhopal Union Carbide Plant Disaster, Bhopal, India, 1984. 2. Chemical industry—Accidents.] I. Title.
HD7269.C452 I52665 2002
363.17'91—dc21
                                                    2002001416

Contents

GREAT DISASTERS
REFORMS and RAMIFICATIONS

Jill McCaffrey
National Chairman
Armed Forces Emergency Services
American Red Cross

Introduction

Disasters have always been a source of fascination and awe. Tales of a great flood that nearly wipes out all life are among humanity's oldest recorded stories, dating at least from the second millennium B.C., and they appear in cultures from the Middle East to the Arctic Circle to the southernmost tip of South America and the islands of Polynesia. Typically gods are at the center of these ancient disaster tales—which is perhaps not too surprising, given the fact that the tales originated during a time when human beings were at the mercy of natural forces they did not understand.

To a great extent, we still are at the mercy of nature, as anyone who reads the newspapers or watches nightly news broadcasts can attest.

7

Hurricanes, earthquakes, tornados, wildfires, and floods continue to exact a heavy toll in suffering and death, despite our considerable knowledge of the workings of the physical world. If science has offered only limited protection from the consequences of natural disasters, it has in no way diminished our fascination with them. Perhaps that's because the scale and power of natural disasters force us as individuals to confront our relatively insignificant place in the physical world and remind us of the fragility and transience of our lives. Perhaps it's because we can imagine ourselves in the midst of dire circumstances and wonder how we would respond. Perhaps it's because disasters seem to bring out the best and worst instincts of humanity: altruism and selfishness, courage and cowardice, generosity and greed.

As one of the national chairmen of the American Red Cross, a humanitarian organization that provides relief for victims of disasters, I have had the privilege of seeing some of humanity's best instincts. I have witnessed communities pulling together in the face of trauma; I have seen thousands of people answer the call to help total strangers in their time of need.

Of course, helping victims after a tragedy is not the only way, or even the best way, to deal with disaster. In many cases planning and preparation can minimize damage and loss of life—or even avoid a disaster entirely. For, as history repeatedly shows, many disasters are caused not by nature but by human folly, shortsightedness, and unethical conduct. For example, when a land developer wanted to create a lake for his exclusive resort club in Pennsylvania's Allegheny Mountains in 1880, he ignored expert warnings and cut corners in reconstructing an earthen dam. On May 31, 1889, the dam gave way, unleashing 20 million tons of water on the towns below. The Johnstown Flood, the deadliest in American history, claimed more than 2,200 lives. Greed and negligence would figure prominently in the Triangle Shirtwaist Company fire in 1911. Deplorable conditions in the garment sweatshop, along with a failure to give any thought to the safety of workers, led to the tragic deaths of 146 persons. Technology outstripped wisdom only a year later, when the designers of the luxury liner *Titanic* smugly declared their state-of-the-art ship "unsinkable," seeing no need to provide lifeboat capacity for everyone onboard. On the night of April 14, 1912, more than 1,500 passengers and crew paid for this hubris with their lives after the ship collided with an iceberg and sank. But human catastrophes aren't always the unforeseen consequences of carelessness or folly. In the 1940s the leaders of Nazi Germany purposefully and systematically set out to exterminate all Jews, along with Gypsies, homosexuals, the mentally ill, and other so-called undesirables. More recently terrorists have targeted random members of society, blowing up airplanes and buildings in an effort to advance their political agendas.

The books in the GREAT DISASTERS: REFORMS AND RAMIFICATIONS series examine these and other famous disasters, natural and human made. They explain the causes of the disasters, describe in detail how events unfolded, and paint vivid portraits of the people caught up in dangerous circumstances. But these books are more than just accounts of what happened to whom and why. For they place the disasters in historical perspective, showing how people's attitudes and actions changed and detailing the steps society took in the wake of each calamity. And in the end, the most important lesson we can learn from any disaster—as well as the most fitting tribute to those who suffered and died—is how to avoid a repeat in the future.

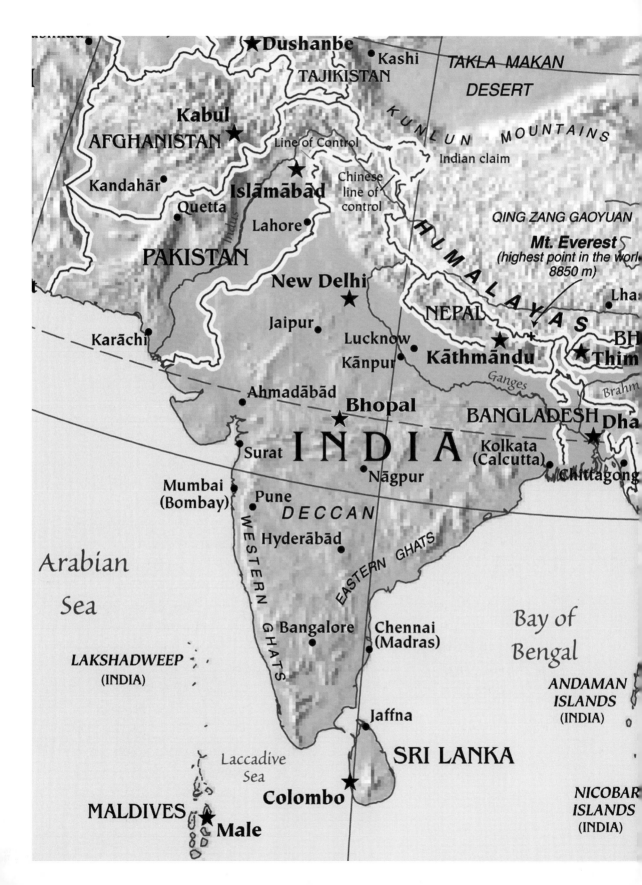

Bhopal is the capital city of Madhya Pradesh, a state in the central part of India. More than 50 million people live in this populous section of the country.

Danger Lies Ahead

As a very large country in southern Asia, India is the second most populated country in the world, next to China, its neighbor to the north. India is filled with jungles and deserts and is one of the places in the world that receives the most rainfall. While the country has many great natural resources, including rich farmlands, most of them have not been sufficiently developed. This has left India with a low standard of living. In fact, many citizens can barely afford the basic necessities of life.

More than 14 major languages and more than 1,000 minor languages and dialects are spoken by the people who live in India. Although some progress has been made in the country, many ways of life in India have stayed the same for hundreds of years. It is not unusual to see ancient customs alongside the latest advances of civilization and science. Cows, which are considered sacred by millions of India's Hindu population, often roam freely in modern business districts.

In the central part of India, more than 50 million people live in the state known as Madhya Pradesh. The capital city, Bhopal, became well known after a terrible chemical accident took place there in the early hours of December 3, 1984. In fact, the Bhopal chemical accident that took place at the Union Carbide plant soon became a massive industrial disaster that affected many people.

Long before that fateful day in 1984, the citizens of India had been reaping the rewards from the employment many had found when Union Carbide opened its first plant in 1940. The company first began producing batteries at a plant it had constructed in Calcutta. Later, Union Carbide began producing flashlights as well. Business was very good because the demand for batteries was at an all-time high, thanks in part to the many electronic toys and radios on sale around the world that worked with batteries.

In the late 1960s, Union Carbide India, Limited (UCIL), had built an additional 13 chemical plants throughout the country. These factories were considered a blessing by many of the people who were employed by them. At one time, Union Carbide India was employing over 10,000 people, who earned an average of 3,000 rupees per month. Although these earnings equaled only $250 in American currency, it was considered an excellent salary by Indian standards.

Union Carbide was so successful that by 1969 it decided to build its fourteenth chemical plant in the northern part of Bhopal. When that plant first opened, it was to be used only to import, package, and distribute raw fertilizer and some pesticide products to other parts of India and East Asia. Everyone who worked at the plant was happy to be employed, and the officials at Union Carbide were happy they had built another profitable factory.

But in 1980, business costs were starting to be a concern to officials at Union Carbide. After several meetings, the administration and top executives of the company decided they would use the Bhopal plant to manufacture pesticides. They were planning on constructing a new production unit at the existing site. For the employees who worked there, this was the beginning of a nightmare they were not prepared for. They would soon learn how to work with and mix dangerous and deadly chemicals.

When word of Union Carbide's plan to start using deadly chemicals at Bhopal reached local officials, they immediately voiced their objections. They were concerned about the potential for a chemical accident that could possibly poison the large population that lived in the areas surrounding the plant. In addition, the railroad station was located only a few miles from the plant; if a chemical accident were to occur, officials were afraid that many more lives would be threatened and harmed. Local officials pleaded with Union Carbide to move their operations to a less populated area.

Despite objections from local officials, many people in the region were looking forward to the additional employment opportunities that would result from the expansion of the Bhopal plant. The expansion from the perspective of Union Carbide seemed only natural, as they had become a powerful industry in the region and they did not want to move operations elsewhere.

Not surprisingly, Union Carbide got their wishes and built the plant that would be able to manufacture the deadly pesticides. The company was confident that the safety measures they had in place would prevent any accidents. But in December 1981, a worker named Mohammed Khan died, and several other employees were injured after being drenched with a deadly gas. Khan and the other employees had been cleaning a pipe

The worst fears of local officials of Bhopal, India, became a reality on December 3, 1984, when a deadly chemical accident at Union Carbide killed 4,000 people. Seventeen years to the day later, a survivor sits beside a sign calling for the arrest of Union Carbide former chairman Warren Anderson.

when the deadly chemical methyl isocyanate (MIC) was released. MIC was one of the ingredients found in the pesticide Sevin™ (carbaril) a widely popular product sold worldwide by Union Carbide. At the Bhopal plant, there were a total of three specially built tanks that held more than 45 tons of MIC.

The accident in 1981, however, was not the first such accident that would plague the Bhopal plant. For example, a routine safety inspection conducted by an American team in 1979 stressed the need for a plan to be put into place that would notify people who lived in the nearby area if a dangerous chemical spill were to happen. A year later, another safety expert said that a disaster plan to evacuate local residents needed to be put into place. However, local officials were never told of these recommendations, and a disaster and evacuation plan was never developed.

Over the next few years, the Bhopal plant continued to operate on a normal basis. There were no major safety or industrial accidents, and plant officials made many changes that had been suggested by the safety experts who had visited there over the past few years. No major chemical leaks had occured, and everyone seemed satisfied with how the operations at the plant were progressing.

The Bhopal plant did have one serious flaw that could eventually cause a major chemical accident, however. The flaw was with its manual backup system, which required that in the event of a pump failure, an employee would need to manually start the backup pump to keep the chemicals from leaking through the pipes. Similar plants in the United States and European countries had the more efficient automatic backup system in place, which meant that if a pump were to fail, a new pump would automatically engage. The automatic backup systems were considered safer and much more efficient than the manual one that was in place at Bhopal. But the Bhopal plant officials actually preferred the manual backup system because it provided additional jobs for local people in the area. More jobs meant that more people could provide for their families and earn a living at the same time.

However, things started taking a turn for the worse in the early part of 1981. Rising prices and the cost of producing the pesticides at the Bhopal plant started to have an impact on Union Carbide. Because Union Carbide had to substantially raise their prices on the pesticides they were selling, many people in the region began to shop around for cheaper products. At the same time, a worldwide interest in how pesticides were affecting the environment was beginning to surface. People were starting to take a second look at how pesticides might be harming wildlife, the earth, and even their own water supplies. Overall, it was beginning to be a

César Chavez, farm labor leader and activist, leads a demonstration in front of a supermarket in Philadelphia, Pennsylvania, on November 14, 1985. The group is protesting the use of pesticides on fresh grapes.

difficult time to be a mass producer of pesticides at a time when cost and environmental issues were starting to be a concern to many consumers, both locally and around the world.

Plant managers began to cut back on costs wherever they felt it was safe to do so. In some cases, employees were told to patch leaky pipes rather than replace them, which was not always a safe idea. To make matters worse, because of the economic problems that the Bhopal plant management was experiencing, they were hiring workers who were underqualified for many crucial positions.

The labor unions at the Bhopal plant did not like how management was handling many safety issues concerning the employees. In 1982, they staged a hunger strike, and Union Carbide responded by firing everyone who was involved. It didn't take long for new workers to be hired, because jobs in the region were almost nonexistent.

The Union Carbide Bhopal plant continued to have

problems with serious accidents. In just over three years, more than 15 workers were injured after they were exposed to several deadly chemicals, including MIC. By 1984, shortly before the world's deadliest industrial and chemical accident was about to take place, the Bhopal plant had seen more than 45 people injured.

Awareness of Safety Problems Grows

Local citizens continued to ignore safety problems at the Bhopal plant. However, local journalists began writing a series of newspaper articles about the safety issues and how it appeared as if Union Carbide was ignoring them rather than fixing them. Several Bhopal chemical workers had quit because of safety concerns.

After some initial investigative reporting, a journalist named Raj Kumar Keswani began to question the Union Carbide safety record—both in the United States and in India. Keswani wrote several newspaper articles that warned of the possibility of a major disaster that could take place at the Bhopal plant in India. He wrote about the high numbers of inexperienced employees who worked there and the concern many of them had for the safety issues. In addition, there were concerns about the many people who lived near the plant. Shortly before the accident would take place in December 1984, it was estimated that more than 125,000 people—nearly 20% of Bhopal's population—lived within a few miles of the plant.

Both government officials and the people of Bhopal ignored the newspaper reporters' warnings, and business at the Union Carbide plant went on as usual. In the last article Keswani wrote about the problems at the Bhopal plant in 1984, he warned of a potential disaster so devastating, no one in the area would live to tell about it. Little did he or anyone else know how true his prediction would become.

An Unthinkable Accident

View of the Union Carbide Bhopal plant, which was the scene of the devastating chemical accident that killed thousands of people and injured tens of thousands in Bhopal, India.

2

On the day of the accident, a worker by the name of Suman Dey arrived for work for his regular night shift at the Union Carbide Bhopal plant. The 26-year-old man was happy to be working at such a facility and considered that what he did was an important job. In fact, many area residents considered it an honor to be employed there. The mood of the people was one of happiness that such a place was located there, which offered so many job opportunities.

Dey had been working at Union Carbide for nearly four years, and although he felt confident in performing his job duties, he knew the dangers and risks in working around such dangerous chemicals. A year earlier, Dey had inhaled a small amount of phosgene gas, which left him hospitalized. He quickly learned that safety precautions needed to be taken, especially when working around such deadly chemicals.

As Dey reported for work, he was happy. Although he had hoped that he would have been promoted long before now, he was still determined to do a good job for his employer. He knew that one day his talents and abilities would be recognized and that he surely would be rewarded.

Dey was not one to cut corners nor to shy away from his duties. If a certain task needed to be accomplished, he would get the job done. On that particular night in December, he saw that a worker on an earlier shift had started cleaning some dirty pipes, but never finished the task. That meant that Dey or someone on his shift would have to be responsible for finishing the job.

From High Pressure to Leak

Apparently, several workers had attempted to clean the dirty pipes, but were unable to complete the job before their shift ended. So Dey took on the responsibility himself. He was familiar with the pipes in the area of the Bhopal plant that needed to be cleaned, and he was resigned to do a good job.

According to later accounts, Dey was not concerned when several of the pressure gauges showed an increase in pressure by almost 8 pounds over a 30-minute period. He knew that the pressure was still within the safe range, so he didn't give it much thought. At about that same time, workers in another part of the plant were assembling and waiting for their nightly orders. Just after 11:30 P.M., one of the workers reported smelling MIC. At first the workers weren't really alarmed, because they had smelled MIC before. As long as the MIC was at low enough levels, it would not pose any serious safety hazards. Nevertheless, the workers immediately set out to find the source of the MIC leak so they could repair it before it got any worse.

Before anyone realized what was taking place, the leak continued to get worse, and the pressure in the pipes where Dey was working rose to dangerous levels. The gauge that had read only 11 pounds just a short time ago was now registering a shocking 45 pounds per square inch. The temperature reading had also risen to almost the top of the scale, and Dey knew that before long the liquid in those pipes would be turning into a deadly gas that would need somewhere to escape.

Within minutes after Dey told his supervisor of the dangerous temperature and pressure readings, the concrete pipe began cracking from the intense heat. With no safety valve strong enough to keep it from escaping, the deadly gas began leaking from the pipe. Just after midnight on December 3, 1984, a chemical accident at the Bhopal plant resulted in the accidental release of approximately 40 metric tons of MIC into the atmosphere. The poison cloud quickly started spreading through the air directly around the huts and shanties that were located near the Bhopal plant. Within minutes, the deadly cloud began silently sneaking up on the unsuspecting residents, as well as many Union Carbide employees.

Numerous Bhopal plant employees tried in vain to contain or neutralize the MIC that was escaping. After various attempts to stop the chemical from spreading, by 1:30 A.M., Dey and the other employees realized that they would not be able to stop the leak. They were afraid for themselves, their fellow employees, and the residents that lived near the Bhopal chemical plant.

By this time most of the employees had put on gas masks, and they were beginning to ask their supervisors if they should begin evacuating the plant. According to published reports, no one thought about sounding an alarm at that point, which would warn the local residents to flee the area. And most people would not have known that a simple wet cloth held over their face and eyes would save their lives.

Just after 2 A.M., an alarm was finally sounded. But the workers were still not ordered to evacuate just yet. Workers without gas masks and breathing devices were told to go to a common meeting area in the plant first. Those with gas masks were asked to remain at their posts, especially anyone working in or near the source of the chemical leak.

Many nearby residents awoke when they heard the alarms coming from the Bhopal plant. Some thought that the Bhopal plant was only testing their alarms, which they had done in years past. Others thought that there was a fire at the plant, and they raced toward the front gate to get a better view. Shortly after arriving near the front gates, the deadly chemical cloud began engulfing the unsuspecting people. Within minutes, these unsuspecting bystanders found themselves coughing uncontrollably while trying to rub the chemical's sting from their eyes. But their efforts were fruitless.

Many employees at the Union Carbide Bhopal plant recognized the smell of the deadly gas but were unable to save themselves. They did not have gas masks close enough to save their own lives. Some of the employees were fortunate enough to know that breathing through a water-soaked cloth, rag, or even an article of clothing would increase their chances for survival.

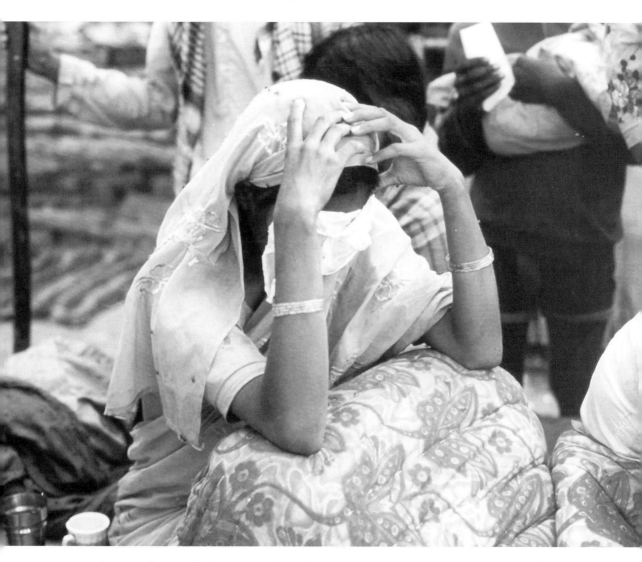

Some of the residents who lived in the shantytowns nearby were Bhopal plant employees. As they woke up to the noise and confusion taking place all around them, they quickly recognized the smell of the deadly gas. One by one employees and their families were awakened from a sound sleep to find themselves in danger. Many screamed, "run for your lives," but by this time the deadly cloud was so large there simply was no place left to escape.

A woman in Bhopal covers her face to protect herself from the poisonous gas that leaked from the Union Carbide factory.

Those residents who were lucky enough to be a few minutes ahead of the deadly chemical cloud were caught in a stampede of hysterical people. People were kicking and stepping on others who had fallen down or who had been pushed in the melée that followed. Chaos continued and large groups of people were literally running around in circles trying to find refuge from the poison gas.

A Train Arrives

About the same time, a train had arrived at the train station, and unsuspecting passengers and their families were going about their normal everyday lives. Despite the lateness of the hour, people were hustling and bustling around as if it were the middle of the day. As people realized they were hearing the alarms sounding at the Bhopal chemical plant, many thought that perhaps there was a fire at the plant. No one had ever suspected a deadly chemical accident had taken place. Within a few minutes, the passengers began to hear the screams of the hordes of people who had been trying to escape from the deadly cloud of poison gas. As the sounds reached the area of the train station and its passengers, so did the deadly cloud of gas. People began choking and rubbing their eyes to try to stop them from stinging so badly. It did not take very long for the scene to go from calm to chaos. Dozens of people began dying.

Fortunately, the stationmaster was able to alert the train's engineer to the perilous situation in and around the Bhopal plant and he pulled the train out of the station before anyone on board was injured or killed. Because it was December, the shutters on the train were closed, and no deadly gas was able to penetrate the cars.

Journalist Keswani Awakens

At the same time that all the chaos was taking place, the journalist, Rajkumar Keswani, woke up in his home at around 1:30 A.M. He was struggling to breathe normally and at first didn't realize what was happening. He had long written warnings of possible chemical leaks at a plant the size of the Union Carbide Bhopal plant, but little did he realize that his warnings were about to turn into a nightmare for everyone in the area.

As Keswani tried to shut the windows of his home, he saw the chaos outside. He witnessed hundreds of people fleeing down the street, and watched in horror as people quickly dropped onto the ground, writhing in pain. He gathered his wife, and together they sat under a fan while he telephoned the local police station. As he asked the dispatcher who answered the telephone what was happening, he was horrified at the response: "It's Union Carbide! A tank has burst and none of us will survive!"

The sudden realization that a nightmare beyond his imagination was taking place before his very eyes was too much for Keswani. All his warnings had fallen on deaf ears, and now everyone was paying the price. But somehow he knew he had to try and save his family from the disaster that was taking place all around them. He and his family lived only about a mile away from the Bhopal plant, and he knew he had to act quickly or everyone would surely die.

With some quick thinking, Keswani told his family to take wet cloths and place them over their faces. His family owned two motor scooters, and he had his brother drive their parents to safety. Keswani then took his wife and his sister on the back of one of the motor scooters. In his anger, however, instead of driving away from Bhopal, he found himself driving toward the Union Carbide plant.

His wife screamed and begged him to turn the other way and drive to safety as quickly as possible. But Keswani was angry, and he could not wait to drive to the Union Carbide Bhopal plant and kill the people that were responsible for allowing the deadly chemicals to leak. Luckily, for him and his family, he started to come to his senses. He realized that if he continued driving so fast in the direction of the Bhopal plant, he was signing his death warrant, and that of his wife and sister. Keswani quickly turned around and drove as fast as the motor scooter would take him to safety. He vowed one day to return and take his revenge on those people responsible for the deadly chemical accident.

Mob Scene at the Hospital

The local hospital filled quickly with people who had somehow managed to get there in hopes of being treated. The Hamidia Hospital was located just less than three miles south of the Union Carbide Bhopal plant, and the first patients had started to arrive just after 1 A.M. They were complaining of chest pains, and they were having trouble breathing and seeing.

As the wind shifted at the Bhopal plant, the deadly gas quickly spread over a wider area, and within a few minutes, about 300 more people arrived at Hamidia Hospital. At about 2:30 A.M., nearly 4,000 people had arrived at the hospital, hoping to be treated. The hospital was not large, having only 750 beds available. Many of the people who made it to the hospital had dropped to the carpet and lay dying.

The medical superintendent of the hospital was Dr. N. R. Bhandari, who was home at the time of the chemical accident. When the staff of the hospital called him for instructions, he was not alarmed. A very confident man, he at first did not think that the chemical leak was anything too serious. He instructed the staff to wash out the patients' eyes and to administer eyedrops, and he assured them that would take care of any of the patients' problems. Feeling that he had adequately taken care of the problem, Dr. Bhandari returned to bed.

Only a few minutes had passed by before Bhandari heard a knock at his front door. Almost a dozen student doctors were coming to his home to ask what had happened. They had not heard anything official about a chemical leak, and they wanted Dr. Bhandari to tell them what to do. Some of the student doctors were beginning to feel the eye irritation, and they wanted instructions on how to best take care of themselves. He immediately told them to wash out their eyes.

As Dr. Bhandari turned on the fans in his home, he called the local police chief, Swaraj Puri. He asked Puri if there had been an excessive number of complaints about anything dangerous in the air. At about the same time, he received the telephone call from the doctor, Police Chief Puri had himself just learned what had happened at the Union Carbide Bhopal plant. He informed the doctor that a gas leak had indeed taken place at the Bhopal plant, and that he was in the process of looking into the situation.

Puri told Dr. Bhandari that the hospital could expect hundreds of people seeking treatment. Little did either man realize how many people would actually end up going to the hospital for help. Because of the way the dangerous cloud was traveling, along with the huge

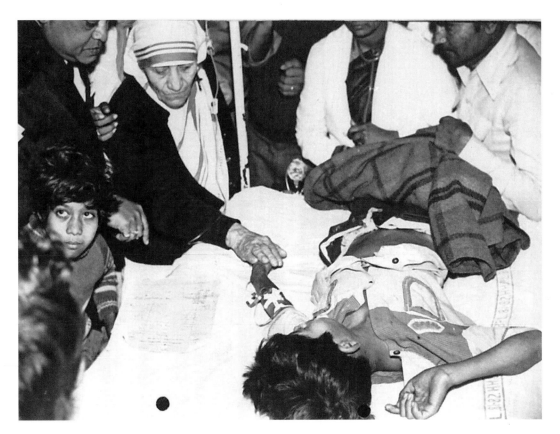

Mother Theresa comforts this victim of the Bhopal chemical disaster in December 1984.

population nearby, by noon the next day an estimated 25,000 people had gone to the hospital for help.

A doctor at Hamidia Hospital described the chaos in these words: "I was standing in the pediatric department. There was such a terrible crowd that there wasn't even a place to keep the bodies on the floor. As soon as a patient was declared dead, his relatives would vanish with the body. I saw at least 50 babies taken away like this. I would estimate that anywhere between 500 and 1,000 bodies were taken away before their deaths could be registered."

By the time dawn had arrived just six or seven short hours after the chemical leak had taken place, countless numbers of people were pouring into hospitals nearby. People were so terrified that mass hysteria had taken over. Countless people were becoming blind and collapsing in the street. The agony of the survivors was best captured in media reports from India, and by those who were able to give their first-hand account of what had taken place. A survivor's words were reported in *India Today*, India's version of *Time Magazine* in the United States, in the February 15, 1985 issue:

> The dead may not have been so unlucky after all. Their end came horribly, it is true, choking on air that had suddenly gone vile. But at least the nightmare was brief. And then it was over. For those who survived the poisonous methyl isocyanate (MIC) leak from the Union Carbide plant, release will not come quickly.
>
> Thousands of the seriously affected survivors have suffered such extensive lung damage that they can no longer apply themselves physically. Their vision often gets blurred, spells of dizziness overtake them, and walking briskly even for a few minutes sends them gasping to their knees, their chests aching. There are women who have peculiar gynecological problems. And there are others—particularly children —who keep reliving those awful hours over and over again.

Survivors' Stories

There were many stories of heroes that surfaced after the tragedy was over. Among three very notable heroes were three employees who worked on the railway. B. B. Sharma, V. R. Dixit, and B. K. Sharma all were on duty when the chemical leak occured. Because the train station is located near the Bhopal plant, they were overcome by the deadly gas fumes, but somehow managed to stay at their posts to prevent other trains from coming in or near Bhopal.

Survivors of the worst chemical disaster in history have recorded their testimonies for future generations to read. Here are just a few first-hand accounts of the horror from that evening:

Fifteen years ago I woke up in the middle of the night crying and coughing. One by one, all the other members in our household got up too with tears streaming down their eyes and something burning their throats. The adults tried to figure out what the unusual smell in the air was but gave up. They closed all the windows and we all went back to sleep.

Of course, I do not remember this incident at all, I was seven months old at the time, but much later, I found out the details. My family and I had been visiting my aunt in Bhopal, India. On the night of December 2, 1984, the Union Carbide Factory at Bhopal sprung a gas leak. Tons of Methyl Iso Cyanate (MIC), hydrogen cyanide, and other lethal gases were released into the air. My parents have told me numerous times about how fortunate we were that the wind had changed direction before much of the gas reached our house. However, there were many who were not as lucky as us.

Official figures stated 1,600 people died in the immediate aftermath of the leak. Realistic figures, which include the many impoverished roadside dwellers with no actual address, are closer to above 8,000. In addition, long term effects of the gases have increased the death toll to over 16,000, with many more still suffering from sicknesses most likely to result in early death. Adequate treatment has not been available for many of the living victims.

In a recent trip to Bhopal, about a year ago, I met a man named Satinath Sarangi (Sathyu). Although he had graduated from college as a metallurgical engineer, he immediately came to help the people in Bhopal after hearing on the radio of the gas leak. Now he has given up his engineering profession and is a trustee of the Sambhavna Trust, an organization dedicated to helping victims of the gas disaster through research and treatment. He has no regrets.

In addition to providing a variety of treatments for the victims, including both standard medical treatment and alternative methods like ayurveda and yoga, the Sambhavna Trust also helps to simply remember the tragedy of the gas leak. The accident had been caused, or at least helped, by carelessness. The Union Carbide factory siren had not gone off; the people had no idea of the danger of the gas until it was upon them, destroying their lungs and other internal organs. Officials at the factory also failed to act quickly, failing to prevent further disaster. It would be careless now, on the fifteenth anniversary of this tragic event, not to remember what happened. In the case of the Bhopal gas leak, it would be best to learn from our mistake.

Sumeet Ajmani
Seabury Hall
102-17 Kaui Place
Kula, HI 96790

I was just eight days old and still in the hospital when the gas leaked. My father who was with me then, told me, doctors put me in a glass box, but I still got gas in my eyes and through my breath. My father also got hit by the gas. My mother and elder sister and brother were at home. They did not run away, all night they stayed under a thick quilt. My mother went out to see what the commotion was all about and she got quite badly affected. She coughs all the time and gets fever often. Her body aches and she has pain in her hands and legs. My father has pain in his stomach. After the gas they kept me in the hospital for about 15 days then all of us went to our village.

I study in fifth grade. Early this year I had gone to my grandmother's place. We had gone for two months but then my uncle broke his leg in an accident so we had to stay longer. When I came back they won't take me back at school. I liked going to school. I used to study Science, Hindi, Social Science and English. Most of all I liked studying science because you learn about how the body works and how things work. When I grow up I want to become a science teacher or a doctor. Most of all I want to become a good man.

I like playing cricket. I think the Indian team is the best in the world and Sachin Tendulkar is the very best. Azharuddin and, Nayan Mongia and Saurav Ganguly are pretty good too. When I play cricket I can't make many runs because I get breathless when I run and my chest hurts. I would like to watch cricket on TV but I cant because my eyes hurt and get filled with tears when I watch TV. My eyes hurt when I read. My friends too have all kinds of health problems. I have many friends but there are about ten with whom I am closest.

We live right across the Carbide factory. So many people in our community are sick. So many have died. And people are still dying after they have been sick for a long time. People cant breathe properly, they often have fever, aches and pain in their stomach. Men and women have become weak. Lots of people cannot go to work.

I do not know who is the owner of the factory. One of my neighbours told me they used to make poisons to kill insects in the factory. I think no body should make poisons. Why kill insects, or rats or any other living thing. They have their life and we have our own. Why kill? The poisons from the factory have come into our drinking water wells. There is poison all around.

This woman is collecting water in front of the Union Carbide plant on February 27, 1985. She and many others living in slum areas around the plant suffer after-effects from the chemical accident.

Some people in my neighbourhood remind me that I stayed alive even though I was so small while so many people died. They make it sound like I brought on all this on the people. That makes me really sad.

Kundan
(8 days old at time of tragedy)

I was ten years old when the gas leaked. In our neighbourhood there was a house where snakes had built their nest. The people in the house used to burn chillies to drive away the snakes. On the night of the gas when all of us woke up coughing and gasping for breath, the first thought that came to our mind was that it was the snake cure gone awry. We opened the door and saw a great number of people all rushing past. Soon we came to know that it was gas coming from Union Carbide's factory. My father said "Lets not run away, because we will surely get separated from each other in this crowd and darkness. If we have to die at least let us die together." All of us were coughing and vomiting and it was getting more and more unbearable. My grandparents had come for a visit, they too were in a miserable state. We opened the door after about four hours. In the morning we went to a tent that had been set up on the roadside and got some medicines from there—eye drops and pills. But these were of no use. My four year old sister Asha died three days after the gas.

My father used to work in a sweet shop making sweets. Ever since the gas he can hardly work. There are times when he thrashes about all night like a fish out of water. Most days he stays in bed. My grandfather used to get very breathless and cough a lot. He suffered this for four years till he died.

I got married when I was seventeen. My husband

used to live in the same neighbourhood. He is a carpenter but can work for hardly fifteen days in a month. He has cough, pain in the chest and can not see properly. He was not given any compensation because he could not present his medical records. During the Hindu-Muslim riots of 1992 his parents' house caught fire and all the papers got burnt. My parents could not get any compensation for the death of my sister and grandfather. The judge asked for papers, but who was thinking of papers three days after the disaster. The officials said that my grandfather did not live in Bhopal and we had to provide documents to show that he was with us on the night of the disaster.

Sharda Vishwakarma
(10 years old at time of chemical leak)

We had had a normal evening at home. I, my four daughter-in laws, my five sons and my daughter. We'd eaten and then gone to sleep. I was the one who woke first. I lay alone in my room and started getting irritated that maybe my daughter-in-laws were burning chillies on the stove. I started shouted and swearing at them. I went to the kitchen where I saw the stove was cold. By this time all my sons and daughter-in-laws had been woken up by my shouting. Smoke started to fill everywhere. Outside people were running and shouting "bhago, bhago." ("Run, run".) We found out from people around that there had been a leak from carbide. We couldn't see anything, we were coughing and kept having loose motions. My grandson was one years old then. I put him on my chest to protect him as much as possible. But his face swelled to twice its size, his eyes were puffed tight. We were really scarred. My daughter-in-law was pregnant then. I could not tell her how deformed her son had become. We thought we were going to die. I kept praying "Allah miah hame bacha lijiye, Allah miah hame bacha lijiye." ("Dear God, please save us, dear Lord, please save us.")

Pretty soon I felt weak and within half an hour I began to pass out. My daughter-in-laws put water on me and tried to get me dressed. They managed to put me in a petticoat. By now, there was so much smoke in the house that we couldn't even see the pots.

Two of my sons had gone to see what had happened. The smaller one was sent back with a message that we should go towards DIG bungalow because there was no gas there. My eyes were now so swollen that I couldn't see out of them. So about an hour after I first felt the gas, we left the house, my daughter-in-laws held me by the hands. The streets were full of corpses. The skins of people were full of blisters. Nobody could be recognised.

We made it to DIG bungalow and then went and sat outside the factory. Many people were there in the same state that we were in. We all just thought of saving ourselves. We stayed there all night and in the morning some doctors came and gave us some red medicine. The military trucks came and took us to "bara sau pachas" ("1250") to the camp.

My daughter who lived near the station sat outside her house with her 20 day old son. She sat there not moving whilst someone came and stole her silver anklet. My son died one month later.

Look at the state of me now. I can't do anything. There has been so much sickness from the gas. I also no longer wear saris. A relative of mine who was wearing a sari got thrown onto a pyre. She was just unconscious. She woke up and ran. Since then no woman in my family wears a sari. We figure that if something else happens to us we should at least be sent off in the proper way (Zubeda Bi is muslim and would wish to be buried). Otherwise people might think we were Hindus and cremate us."

Zubeda Bi
(46 years old when the
chemical leak occurred)

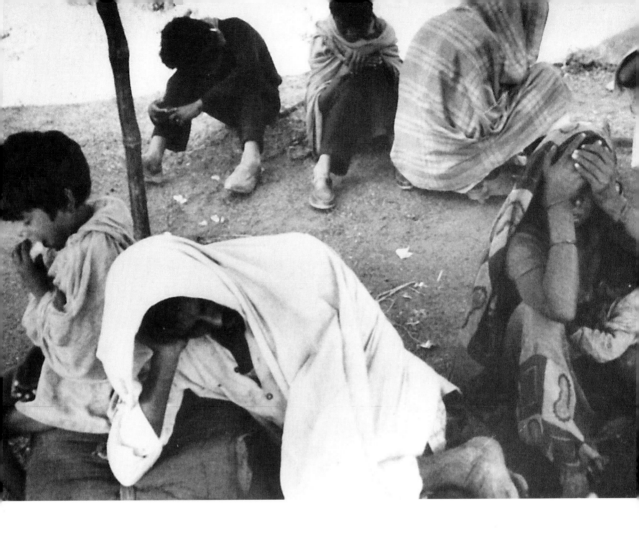

What
Happened
Next

Some of the thousands of people injured by breathing harmful air from a poisonous chemical leak from the Bhopal Union Carbide plant are waiting to be treated. Most common injuries among survivors are shortness of breath, red eyes, and nausea.

3

As the seriousness of the tragedy began to sink into the minds of everyone who had been in the middle of this unspeakable crisis, there were many questions: "What had happened?" "What kind of a chemical leak was this? "Why were so many people dying?" "Isn't there anything we can do to stop the killing?"

Examining the Dead

The head of the forensic medicine and toxicology department at Gandhi Medical College was a doctor named Hireesh Chandra. He was home sleeping soundly while all of the chaos was taking place. But he was awakened at around 5:30 A.M. and informed of what was happening. He quickly went to the hospital with a colleague, and both were shocked at what they saw there. They could not imagine what was causing so many people to be affected at the same time. Dr. Chandra directed another doctor to start performing autopsies on several of the victims. He wanted to find out what was causing everyone to die, in hopes that he might prevent other people from dying unnecessarily.

While the other doctors were performing autopsies on the bodies that had already perished, Dr. Chandra was busy researching everything he could about the chemical MIC. Because there was so little information about MIC in the hospital library, he wasn't able to learn anything really new. He realized that MIC, which by itself was not supposed to be deadly, had somehow managed to cause death and destruction among so many innocent people.

As Chandra himself began performing autopsies on some victims who had passed away, he was shocked to find that many had thick, cherry-red blood and lungs that were ash covered. He also detected a scent of bitter almonds, which is the odor of cyanide, which would explain that these people had somehow died of cyanide poisoning. He then wondered if the MIC had mixed with the water in people's bodies to produce hydrocyanide as well as a combination of other deadly gases. During the first 24 hours after the chemical spill, Dr. Chandra had assembled a small team of doctors who spent hours performing over 150 autopsies. Each time they examined a victim of the tragedy, they found the same results: what seemed to be plain evidence that the patient had died from cyanide poisoning.

Over the next few hours chaos continued. Rumors were being spread by everyone. No one really knew the truth about what had happened, because at the time even the employees at the Union Carbide Bhopal plant still were not sure what had taken place.

Back inside the Hamidia Hospital, the dead bodies were first placed in the morgue. However, owing to the large numbers of people who passed away, the morgue quickly filled up, and doctors, nurses, and other volunteers at the hospital began placing the cadavers outside on the lawn.

Not Really Dead

It was reported that some of the people who were declared dead were done so accidentally. Several books written about the Bhopal tragedy tell of a man named Sayed Abbas, who was declared dead and then placed in the hospital morgue. About 5:30 in the morning, Abbas regained consciousness and suddenly realized where he was. Because the morgue was kept at a very cold temperature to preserve the bodies, it was freezing and Abbas was only covered with a sheet. However, the bodies that had been placed all around him and literally on top of him had kept him warm. So when he woke up, he grabbed his sheet and ran out of the morgue. Several guards who had been assigned to keep people from entering the morgue in search of their loved ones were startled and thought for sure that someone had "risen from the dead!"

Another bizarre story tells of Munnibai Balkishensingh, a woman who worked at the local rail station as the water woman. After she was overcome by the deadly fumes, she passed out and people mistook her for one of a dozen of dead bodies that they had stumbled across. She was eventually placed in a large pile of bodies that apparently had no heartbeat and were presumed to be dead. Local health officials were afraid of an epidemic of cholera if the corpses were not immediately cremated. So when a doctor could detect no sign of a heartbeat from Munnibai, she was placed on a truck with a large number of dead bodies and taken away to be part of a mass cremation. Luckily for Munnibai, as soon as the wood was lit on fire and she was about to be burned alive, someone noticed her foot beginning to move. A man who was standing nearby quickly grabbed her and pulled her body out of the flames. She was lucky enough to be taken to a local hospital, where she recovered.

Too Many Injured, Too Few Doctors, and Too Few Supplies

Because of their limited medical facilities, no hospital in the area was prepared to treat the 20,000 people who sought treatment and help from their misery and pain. Patients kept coming through the doors, and it didn't take long for the staff to be overwhelmed and out-numbered. People could not be seen because there was literally no room in the waiting rooms, the treatment rooms, or any of the wards. Many patients ended up on the lawns in front of the hospitals. Some died there, a swift and painful death, while others, still writhing in pain, continued to lie there for hours and hours, waiting for someone—anyone—to come and make their pain go away.

According to published reports from the Indian Council of Medical Research, "between eight and ten thousand people were treated at Hamidia Hospital for eye problems on the first day, including for 'intense burning of the eyes, profuse lacrimation, photophobia and blepherospasm, and visual disturbances.' Others suffered from intense gastritis, burning sensations, vomiting, and diarrhea, and many patients lapsed into unconsciousness, asphyxia and coma."

Shortages of medical supplies and equipment were

apparent because of the large numbers of patients seeking treatment for their pain and suffering. In addition, most of the local medical doctors and nurses had limited knowledge of MIC and how to treat patients who had been exposed to it. They did have the literature that Union Carbide had provided, but none of the literature ever mentioned a disaster of this magnitude as a distinct possibility.

Despite the doctors' efforts to treat everyone, there were simply not enough medical supplies to ensure, for example, that each person would have a clean syringe, so needles were used over and over again, which greatly increased the patients' risk of infection. But that was a risk the doctors were willing to take, and

On December 10, 1984, Alan W. Johns, OBE Director, Royal Commonwealth Society for Blind England, (*center*) arrives in India to discuss how to treat the injured with Dr. Rajenora Vyas (*right*) and Dr. Kerr Muir (*left*). There is great concern about blindness among survivors.

they felt the danger of infection was far less than the danger of the chemical reaction that many people were experiencing at the time.

There were also inadequate supplies of neosporin, which normally is an effective eye medication. The hospital at Hamidia only had 100 cylinders of oxygen on hand, along with just a few respirators. "How could they possibly expect to treat so many patients who kept coming and coming and who obviously needed to be treated for damage to their lungs," the doctors and nurses kept asking.

For several days following the chemical leak, there were conflicting reports as to how many people had become victims of the tragedy. According to unofficial estimates, it was reported that about 100,000 people had been affected by the gas in one way or another. That included people who had been directly in the path of the escaping deadly gas, as well as people who had inhaled or consumed fruits and vegetables or water that had been affected by the gas. There were also conflicting numbers reported by the local government officials. According to the author of *A Killing Wind: Inside Union Carbide and the Bhopal Catastrophe* "two years after the catastrophe, the government would say about 2,500, but evidence points to a figure closer to 8,000."

Several investigations by officials, Union Carbide representatives, Red Cross, and other organizations all revealed different numbers of people who had been affected by the chemical leak. According to various crematorium records, approximately 3,000 Hindu bodies were burned in the 18 months after the accident. Local evidence concluded that by early 1986 about 8,000 people died from the direct effects of the gas. But the government refused to include deaths that took place long after the accident.

Because of the numbers of casualties, death certificates were not filed for everyone who passed away that fateful evening. There was simply not enough time for the doctors to complete any type of paperwork; they were too busy trying to save lives and treat the wounded and ill. This partly explains the differences in the numbers of people who should have been counted as direct casualties of the deadly chemical accident at the Bhopal plant.

Engineers from another nearby company, Bharat Heavy Electricals, Ltd., were able to enter the Union Carbide Bhopal plant, find the leak, and repair it. However, even though it was only about an hour after the leak had started, all the deadly gas had escaped.

Throughout the streets bodies continued to pile up, along with the decomposing bodies of water buffalo and even cattle. By the next morning, several construction cranes were sent to remove the debris, people, and animals that lay dead in the streets.

Warren M. Anderson, chairman of the board of Union Carbide at the time of the disaster, speaks to the media on December 10, 1984. He acknowledges previous safety problems in the plant in India, but does not acknowledge that these problems have any connection to the poisonous gas leak.

Union Carbide Responds

4

B ecause there were only two telephone trunk lines serving the central Indian city of more than 750,000 people, information was slow to arrive and often came in bits and pieces. During the first few hours after they had been informed of the incident, people had to rely on BBC radio news reports coming out of New Delhi and Bombay.

By the time news of the chemical accident and its aftermath made its way to the United States and to Union Carbide's headquarters, it was already afternoon in India. The chairman of Union Carbide was Warren M. Anderson, and he received a telephone call informing him of the chemical leak.

Union Carbide Talks to the Media

At 1 P.M. EST (Eastern Standard Time) on December 3, 1984, Union Carbide officials held their first official press conference at the Danbury

Hilton hotel in Connecticut. They kept their first press conference relatively short and held to the facts that they could confirm: Yes, a chemical accident had taken place at a plant owned by Union Carbide India, Ltd., in which they owned a 50.9% share. Officials explained how they were dispatching medical teams and teams of technical experts to help contain and dispose of any remaining chemicals. They also announced that they were halting production at their only other facility where MIC was being produced at a plant in West Virginia. They stressed that they would keep everyone informed of new information as soon it was received and confirmed. At that point, rumors were still flying as to what had happened and how many people had actually been killed or injured.

Over the next few days Union Carbide officials kept holding press conferences to keep everyone informed of what was happening in Bhopal and nearby communities. Press coverage of the Bhopal chemical accident was intense. They had to respond to hundreds of media inquiries from countries the word over. Major newspapers from all around the world carried the Bhopal chemical accident as a front-page breaking news story. For weeks after the incident, newspapers and magazines kept the story alive because there were so many stories to tell. Eventually, though, the media coverage turned from one of "disaster and survivor" coverage to a story that would become a complex legal drama. Scientists and engineers from around the world lent their expertise to try and get to the cause of the chemical leak.

Policies for Dealing with the Accident

In response to the many questions, both from the media and government agencies, Union Carbide did implement some important policies rather quickly.

- The West Virginia plant that manufactured MIC was quickly closed and stayed closed until safety measures were reexamined and more became known about the cause of the Bhopal tragedy.

- A management task force was formed headed by chairman of the board of Union Carbide, Warren Anderson. The management task force took on the role of dealing with the Bhopal crisis head on.

- Chairman Anderson, in an effort to show how much the company cared, took full responsibility for the terrible tragedy, and accepted moral responsibility for the incident at a December 4th news conference. He announced that he and a team would be traveling to India at once to offer $1 million in aid to the victims.

- A medical and technical team was dispatched to the Bhopal scene within 24 hours of the incident. Their goal was to arrange for immediate and long-term relief, to assist in the safe disposal of any remaining MIC supplies at the plant, and to investigate the cause of the accident.

According to the Jackson Browning Report by the Union Carbide Corporation, "Because of the obstacles placed in our way by Indian authorities, it would be March 1985 before we could point with certainty to the cause. In the interim, we took the heat."

Union Carbide, like most major corporations, did have a contingency plan for emergencies. The plan called for the step-by-step framework and offered guidelines on how to respond to emergencies. But no plan had ever prepared the Union Carbide officials, or anyone else for that matter, for the tragedy at the Bhopal plant in India.

The long hours, dedication, and efforts by many company employees helped Union Carbide to deal with what had taken place. Union Carbide had earned the trust, respect, and admiration of many people, and they wanted to show the world they were going to take responsibility for the disaster and fix all future problems. Union Carbide knew that they had to deal with the problem of any leftover MIC in the plant before any further incidents or accidents could take place. But their efforts to send in a technical team of experts were blocked at first by the Indian government. The Indian government, along with local residents, did not trust Union Carbide at this point. Everyone was afraid that something terrible would happen again, just by simply letting a technical team go into the plant.

Union Carbide was finally able to convince the Indian government that it was absolutely necessary to send in a technical team to convert any remaining MIC into a less volatile compound. "Operation Faith" was soon launched. However, hordes of people demanded to be evacuated from the Bhopal area before it would take place. The Indian military sent several planes filled with water overhead of the Bhopal plant. They were ready on a moment's notice to drop water over any chemical cloud that might contain the deadly mixture of MIC.

Anderson's Visit to Bhopal

On December 7, an Indian Airlines jet landed at Bhopal's Bairagarh Airport with Warren Anderson and a team of colleagues. Anderson had decided not to use the corporate jet to keep a low profile. He did not want to appear that he was a rich corporate leader

View of the general office buildings and skyscraper of Union Carbide in New York City, New York.

who was uncaring about what had happened to the people in and around Bhopal. As the team departed the plane, they were met by a band of police officers. At first, Anderson thought they were simply being offered a police escort as a security precaution. As the door to the airplane was opened, the police officers entered and asked for Mr. Anderson, Mr. Mahindra, and Mr. Gokhale to please stand up and step forward. Everyone else was told to remain in their seats for the time being.

As the three men exited the plane, they were met by Police Superintendent Swaraj Puri and District Collector Moti Singh. They were then directed to a car that had been driven onto the tarmac near the airplane. The car sped away and left through a side gate to avoid the hordes of media that had gathered to cover their arrival.

A few minutes later, the car arrived at a guesthouse, and the three men were directed to a suite of rooms that were usually reserved for VIPs. Anderson and his companions noted that there were over three dozen police officers standing guard around the building. At that point, the police officers told Anderson and the others that they were under arrest.

Anderson asked what the charges were, and he was told they were being placed under house arrest for their own protection. The police said they were not sure they could guarantee their safety if they were allowed to roam the streets by themselves. Anderson was told that his meeting with Chief Minister Singh would be allowed to take place later that day. At about 11 A.M. that morning, Police Superintendent Puri returned with Chief Minister Singh and they brought with them a city magistrate. The Union Carbide executives thought for sure they were about to be released. Instead, they were shocked when they were told that the city magistrate was there to file charges against them.

The charges included culpable homicide not amounting to murder; culpable homicide causing death by negligence; mischief in the killing of livestock; making the atmosphere noxious for health; and negligent conduct with respect to poisonous substances. Anderson was worried, because he knew those first two charges carried a penalty of life imprisonment.

Later that day Anderson was released and allowed to return to the United States. At first, he refused to leave without his two companions, men whom he had known for years. But they convinced him that he should go, because he would be able to do more good back in the United States than as a prisoner in Bhopal. Reluctantly, Anderson agreed and was allowed to go free.

New Legislation

Both Union Carbide and the government of India sponsored investigations into the incident. However, both Union Carbide and the government of India were parties to the associated lawsuit. As a result, very few issues about the incident were not in dispute. For example, both parties agreed that the MIC release was due to a violent reaction from the inappropriate introduction of water into the storage tank. How the water reached the tank and the capacity of the plant to safely handle this problem were issues addressed in the trial.

In 1985, the Government of India passed the Bhopal Gas Leak Disaster Act. This act made the government of India the representative for all individuals seeking compensation from the incident. When the cases were combined in the U.S. court system, there were approximately 145 actions involving 200,000 plaintiffs. In 1986, the U.S. District Court of southern New York found in favor of Union Carbide and directed that the trial be moved to India.

The government of India contended that Union Carbide was actively involved in the detailed plant design and that while finalizing the plant design Union

Carbide intentionally reduced or eliminated safety items. During plant operation the Indian government claimed that Union Carbide failed to ensure that appropriate maintenance was performed on the Bhopal plant's infrastructure or that the recommendations of safety audit teams were implemented. For example, the MIC should have been vented through a scrubber and flare tower before exiting the facility, but a leaking vent line released the MIC directly to the atmosphere. Moreover, the MIC that did reach the scrubber was not removed because neither the scrubber nor the flare tower was operational at the time of the incident. (If all the MIC reached the scrubber, and the scrubber and flare tower were operational, however, there may still have been a release, since it is believed that the venting MIC would have exceeded the scrubber design capacity.)

Union Carbide disputed these claims, stating that although it had provided the basic MIC unit design to Union Carbide India, Ltd., the government of India had prohibited Union Carbide's active participation in the final plant design. Union Carbide asserted that it had provided appropriate training, which included sending some workers to Institute, West Virginia for training. Moreover, Union Carbide contended that Union Carbide India, Ltd., management was generally responsible for safety and maintenance at the plant and that the government of India was the responsible regulator of the plant. Ultimately, after reviewing the plant records, interviewing plant employees, and studying the incident, Union Carbide concluded that the MIC storage tank was sabotaged.

The trial ended in 1989 when the Supreme Court of India ordered Union Carbide and Union Carbide India, Ltd., to pay $470 million in damages to the government of India. The settlement was challenged

The Chairman and chief executive officer of Union Carbide, Robert D. Kennedy, speaks to stockholders about the settlement against Union Carbide of America and Union Carbide of India to pay damages to the government of India in 1989.

in 1991. The courts upheld the civil settlement, but allowed the criminal case to be reopened. The criminal case remains open today, and Union Carbide has sold its stake in Union Carbide India, Ltd.

In August 1985, the Union Carbide sister plant in Institute, West Virginia, released a cloud of methylene chloride and aldicarb oxide that affected four neighboring communities and led to the hospitalization of over 100 people. In the wake of this and the Bhopal incident,

Congress passed the 1986 Emergency Planning and Community Right to Know Act. This act, implemented by the Environmental Protection Agency (EPA), facilitates state and local accident contingency planning, public participation, and access by individuals and communities to information regarding hazardous materials in their locales.

In 1990, while developing the Clean Air Act Amendments, the Senate considered an EPA analysis that compared U.S. chemical incidents in the early to mid 1980s with the Bhopal incident. Of the 29 incidents considered, 17 incidents in the United States involved release of sufficient volumes of chemicals with such toxicity that the potential consequences (depending on weather conditions and plant location) could have been more severe than in Bhopal. Based on the incident review and existing state and federal programs, the Senate concluded that accident prevention had not been given sufficient attention in the existing federal programs.

After reviewing the analysis by the EPA, the Senate wrote amendments to the Clean Air Act that assigned the task of developing programs to prevent chemical incidents to the EPA and the Occupational Safety and Health Administration (OSHA). Congress authorized the EPA to promulgate the Risk Management Program Rule for protection of the public and authorized OSHA to promulgate the Process Safety Management Standard to protect workers. The two programs share a requirement for covered facilities to develop accident prevention plans; other provisions are complementary. The amendments also established the independent U.S. Chemical Safety and Hazard Investigation Board.

Using the National Transportation Safety Board as a model, the amendments assigned the Board the task of investigating and reporting on the causes and probable causes of domestic chemical incidents. Moreover, the Senate recommended that the Board provide investigative assistance to other countries both as a means of helping and as a means of learning. Through its international outreach efforts to government and industry, the National Transportation Safety Board can ensure its safety research program, professional services, and technical information accurately and adequately address the world's chemical safety.

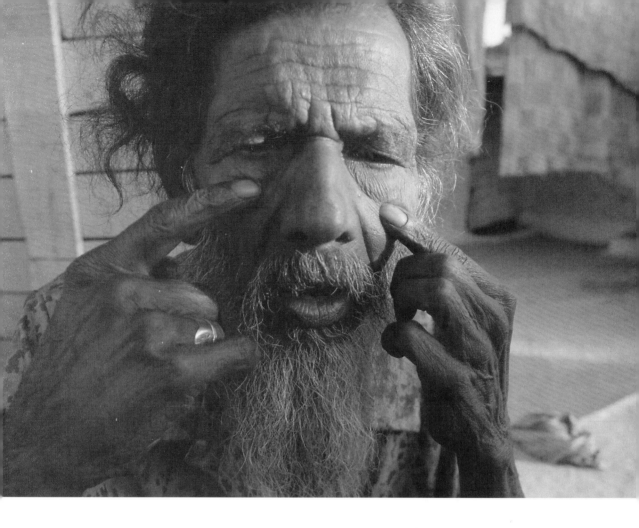

A Long Period of Suffering

Victim of chemical acci-
dent at Bhopal indicates
that he is blind as a result
of the chemical leak
(photo taken in 1989).

5

A team of at least 50 scientists and engineers from India were on hand to supervise the processing of MIC into a less harmful pesticide product. Once Operation Faith was completed and the Union Carbide Bhopal plant was declared safe again, the local residents felt for the first time that they were out of danger. They wanted to go on with their lives, mourn for their dead, and try to rebuild a life somehow that would make all of the madness go away.

There are hundreds, if not thousands, of stories of people that were affected by the chemical disaster. Here are a few that have been posted on a website (www.Bhopal.org):

Name: Sajida
Age at Disaster: 6 years old

I was in the first grade at the time of the gas disaster. I remember being woken up by people in my family. I remember everyone vomiting and groaning and then joining the crowd of people who were trying to run away from the clouds of poison. Since then my problem of breathlessness has been getting worse, my eye problems are also getting worse and now everything appears blurry. I am also getting more and more weak. I was very keen on studying but I failed my exams in the eighth grade. I was very sick at the time of the examination. I told my teacher that I could not write my exams because of my illness but she refused to take my application for leave of absence.

So I failed and that was the end of my studies. I have never stopped regretting this. When I see other women pursuing their studies I wish I had continued. Since I was a child I wanted to do something important, become someone famous and I still can not accept that none of my wishes will ever come true. Now I spend most of my time doing chores at home and some embroidery work with "zari." My eyes go blurred when I work with "zari."

It's been over 10 years since I have been so sick. I have been admitted to the hospital several times. My elder brother Rayees used to be so breathless; he had to sit through the whole night. His lungs were badly damaged. He died four years back. He died in the hospital. I think of him often and the one thing I feel really bad about is that I was not there by his side when he died. My father owned a truck and three auto-rickshaws. He sold them one by one to pay for

Rayees' medical bills. Now my father rents an autorickshaw for the day and our family survives on what he makes.

For the last one month he has been sick in bed and I am taking care of household expenses through my "zari" work. My mother Aneesa too is sick. She is breathless has chest pain and pain in the stomach and she has swelling in her limbs. She has a fever that never leaves her.

Name: Razia Bee
Age at Disaster: 26 years old

We were sleeping peacefully that night. I got up to find the children vomiting all over. First I wondered whether it was some thing they had for dinner. Then I too started vomiting. Soon all of us, my husband and me carrying the children were running towards Lily Talkies. My three-year-old daughter Nazma had swelled up so much like she would burst. We took her to Hamidia hospital. We stayed with her at the hospital for 15 days and then the doctors said she would not survive. We were feeling so utterly helpless because there was no doctor around who knew how my baby could be saved. She died on the fifteenth day.

My husband Rafique owned a watch repair shop. After the gas he suffered the most in our family. He would need to sit under a fan. His mouth stayed open and he had those violent coughing bouts. Often he would cough blood. He was admitted to Hamidia hospital for three weeks and then sent home. Soon after early one morning at 3 am he started vomiting and it would not stop. So we took him back to Hamidia. After a month of his being in

One year after the Bhopal chemical leak, people still line up outside Hamidia Hospital for treatment of their injuries.

the hospital the doctors said now take him home we can't do anything to help your husband. I had bitter arguments with the doctors but finally brought my husband home. Then a Red Cross hospital was set up near our house.

One month he took treatment there and then the doctor there said these drugs are not doing you any good, you might as well stop taking them. So I took him to the government's Shakir Ali hospital but the treatment there did little good. Though we were supposed to get free medicines the doctor there said if you want to get better medicines you should buy them from the market. One morning the doctor wrote a prescription and I worried all day about where to get Rupees five hundred to but all the medicines. My husband died the same evening at 4 o clock.

Meanwhile we had had to sell off the watch repair shop at a very low price. I went to the claim court with my husband's medical papers but the officials there said you have to get the "04 form" filled. They told me to come later in December ('92) But by then the city was aflame with Hindu-Muslim riots. I was not able to receive any compensation for my husband's death nor for my daughter Nazma's.

My daughter Salma developed strange symptoms. She would itch all over her body and get round blue marks as big as a rupee coin. I took her to Hamidia then to Shakir Ali where they told me to take her to Indore. By then she was in a very bad state. She had high fever and her tear drops were red coloured. Also she complained of her head aching all the time. I took her to the government hospital in Jehangirabad where even after four months of regular treatment there was no improvement in her condition. Then I took her to a private clinic. They told me right in the beginning that Salma's treatment will be long and expensive. I had no money left so I brought my daughter back. But then her condition worsened and I went back to the private clinic. At the end of her treatment Salma was only slightly better and I was in debt for Rs 50, 000. Till today we have not been able to pay back all the money.

Finally Salma got treated at the Sambhavna clinic where with Ayurvedic treatment she got much better. I too have been very sick after the gas. I do not remember falling sick before the gas. To keep the home fire going I did all kinds of jobs—sweeping, washing dishes and every kind of hard labour. My vision is blurred, I loose my balance while walking, I get very breathless and get panic attacks. When I tell my problems to the doctors at the government hospitals they say you are just making all these up. None of my children could study. Only my daughter Sazida has passed eigth grade in the government school. The school is supposed to be free but the teachers find ways to get money from the students.

Name: Jewan Shinde
Age at Disaster: 32 years old

I used to be an autorickshaw driver and around 12.30 am on the night of the disaster I was driving through Bharat Talkies going towards home. I suddenly started feeling really hot. At that time I could not see any signs of the gas or the turmoil of afterwards. I got home and went to sleep not thinking anything more. Around 2.30 am I suddenly awoke to find that my quilt was on the floor despite it being a winters night. Outside there was screaming and shouting of "bhago, yaha se bhago." ("Run, run away from here.") There used to be a food inspector who lived opposite our house and I could hear his voice outside. From inside the house I shouted asking him what was going on. He shouted back that gas had leaked from Carbide and that I should not open the door. By this time smoke had started seeping through from under the door. That was when the coughing started. I, my wife and my two sons (aged 4 & 6 at that time) felt as if we were choking.

It felt like someone was burning chillies. I got really scared and out of fear I opened the door. Outside everyone was running, screaming, nothing could be seen—the thick fog hung everywhere. It was clear that we were being poisoned—the stench of rotting potatoes was strong. I took my family to the landlords house who stayed one door away. The gas filled their house also. 14 people, my family and my landlord's family then all climbed into my autorickshaw and I started going towards new market. I, by mistake took the wrong road—instead of going towards the cantonement, I headed through Qazi Camp. Everywhere there were people running, vomiting, men and women wearing almost nothing. The cloud still hung thick. Many people tried stopping the auto and begged for space, but what could I do? Driving through Qazi camp I started to feel faint and I thought I would lose consciousness. My landlords wife, Rama Devi kept saying "himat rakho, is gadi ko bahar nikalna hai." ("Have courage, we've got to get this vehicle out of here.")

Terror had filled me from within. Street lamps looked as if they were dim candles burning. Peoples screams and shouts dulled by the thickness of the gas fog. By the time we made it to Kamla Park it seemed the gas was over. I then took my family to South T.T Nagar where someone known to Rama Devi lived.

I then tied a wet muffler over my mouth and went back into the city to find out what had happened. If I had known how poisonous the gas was then I would not have gone. I can not tell you what state people were in. Almost undressed. I saw an old woman at the government offices in a sari blouse and shorts just sitting. Bodies strewed the streets.

At around 4 am a man stopped me and asked me to take him to the station. I told him that all trains had stopped. But he insisted. We got to the station. Five corpses lay on Platform five. The man saw this and ran.

All night I roamed in my auto. Picking up as many people as I could, those who fell against my auto and dropped them wherever I could. The roads were full of people. The stampede of the dead and living. Police vans were roaming blaring "vacuation." I saw a dead buffalo, twice the usual size. Its tail stuck straight up into the air.

At around 6 am I made it back to my house in Teela Jamalpura. The whole colony was desolate, apart from a few people who had not run. Most of them were vomiting outside their own homes. I opened the door of my house and thick gas started coming out. I left the door open and ran again.

I made it back to South T.T Nagar where my family was. By the time I got home my eyes were swollen and were red like tomatoes. By 10.30 that morning I took my wife and children and went back home. I will never forget what I have seen.

Settlement Money Sent by Union Carbide Officials

Within a few days of the chemical disaster, Union Carbide officials began sending money for relief efforts. They gave $1 million directly to the Indian government and gave the Red Cross another $5 million to handle relief efforts that were taking place in the Bhopal region. The Indian government offered a settlement of 10,000 rupees (only $830.00) to each family who lost a loved one.

Lawyers Get Involved

In the days, weeks, and months following the chemical disaster at the Bhopal plant, dozens of lawyers decided that they wanted to get involved. In fact, at one time there were so many lawyers running around Bhopal looking for clients to represent that the local India media referred to the incident as "The Great Ambulance Chase."

Many of the lawyers who traveled to Bhopal wanted their lawsuits to be filed in the United States rather than India. They felt strongly that they could win larger amounts of money for their clients there, and in less time as well.

Prime Minister Rajiv Ghandi attends a rally in December 1984 by and for survivors of the Union Carbide plant accident.

A Look at Bhopal Today

6

Much has happened in Bhopal since that fateful night of the tremendous chemical accident in December 1984. Thousands of lives were lost, and thousands more would become affected with a wide range of medical problems for years to come. While experts, governments, businesses, and individuals all disagree on whom to blame and what should be done, the one thing that everyone agrees on is that it should not be allowed to happen again.

According to the Jackson Browning Report, written by Union Carbide Vice President Jackson B. Browning, many significant events took place after the chemical leak. He writes:

In 1985, the government of India filed a civil suit against Union Carbide in Federal District Court in New York City—after it had quickly enacted a law giving it the right to represent all Bhopal victims and the exclusive right to teach a settlement on their behalf. The Indian government had hired an American law firm, pursing its strategy to try the case in the U.S. courts where it presumably hoped for a higher award or settlement than could be expected in India. At one point in 1986, a settlement with attorneys in the United States seemed imminent, but lawyers representing the government would not agree and the deal fell apart. Eventually the U.S. courts established that India was the proper site for any Bhopal action and sent the litigation there for disposition.

Union Carbide knew it had a responsibility to take care of the victims. The company publicly took moral responsibility for the incident that took place at the Bhopal plant in India. They also offered more than $20 million in relief aid that would be above and beyond any settlement figures or damages. As an additional way to help the people of Bhopal, Union Carbide announced that they were giving a $2.2 million grant to Arizona State University to establish a vocational-technical training center for Bhopal's citizens.

Union Carbide has attempted to take care of the victims of the tragedy ever since it took place. Beginning with the days immediately following the accident, Union Carbine's aid to the victims of Bhopal has continued over the last 16 plus years. And the employees of Union Carbide were so deeply moved by the victims and their problems that they created an employees' relief fund that collected more than $100,000 for the Bhopal people.

The company also sent additional medical supplies and equipment to Bhopal in an effort to help local medical personnel deal with the many problems afflicting the people. And in June of 1985, Union Carbide contributed funds for Indian medical experts to attend meetings on research and treatment to victims. By January 1986, Union Carbide Corporation and Union Carbide India, Ltd., offered the Indian government $10 million to build a hospital to aid the victims of the Bhopal tragedy.

For the next 10 years, petitions were filed in various courts, both in the United States and in India. Finally, on February 15, 1989, the Supreme Court of India directed a final settlement of all Bhopal litigation in the amount of $470 million to be paid by March 31, 1989.

Union Carbide did not stop there. In April 1992, Union Carbide established an independent charitable trust for a Bhopal hospital and announced plans to sell its interest in the Bhopal plant. It took several court actions before the groundbreaking of the new hospital took place in the middle of October 1995. Currently, the building has been completed, but new equipment is still being installed and staff is still being selected. The hospital is expected to have the necessary facilities for the treatment of eye, lung, and heart problems.

The Official Settlement

According to the official website posted by the Union Carbide Corporation, the following information contains the details of the official settlement terms:

> The $470 million final settlement is many times larger than any damage award in the history of India. It is also $120 million more than the $350 million settlement accepted by U.S. attorneys representing

the Indian victims in the U.S. Courts. U.S. attorneys sued in American courts for more than $50 billion. They ultimately told the U.S. court that $350 million was a fair settlement. The Supreme Court of India ruled that the $470 million settlement was "just, equitable and reasonable." The court reached this conclusion after a review of U.S. and Indian court filings, applicable law and facts, and an assessment of the needs of the victims.

According to a Press Trust of India report, the government of India submitted proof to the Supreme Court of India that the $470 million settlement would provide $3.1 billion, if invested at 10 percent interest compounded for 20 years—the amount of time India's Attorney General estimated it would take for a suit as hotly contested as the Carbide case to be tried and decided.

Settlement by order of the Supreme Court of India was the only feasible outcome, according to many legal authorities. Union Carbide Corporation had strong legal defenses to the government of India's claims. As a U.S. appeals court concluded, ". . . the (Bhopal) plant has been constructed and managed by Indians in India." Neither the victims nor UCC would gain by continuing litigation into the 21st Century.

On May 4, 1989, the Supreme Court of India, in a long opinion, explained the rationale for the settlement. The court emphasized that the compensation levels provided for in the settlement were well in excess of those that would ordinarily be payable under Indian law.

Taking the average amount per victim for each victim category used by the Supreme Court of India in its May 4, 1989, opinion and the number of victims

in each category in the completed categorization of claims reported by the State Government of Madhya Pradesh on November 30, 1990, the portion of the settlement fund needed to compensate the victims is 4.8 billion rupees. On November 14, 1990, the Reserve Bank of India reported that the settlement fund with interest was then 8.57 billion rupees.

Union Carbide's information about the processing and settlement of claims is limited to sporadic media coverage. Such articles have indicated that about two-thirds of the claims have been decided and about

Survivors of the Bhopal gas disaster do not believe that they have been treated fairly by the United States. To illustrate this, on September 2, 2000, protesters carry a coffin meant to represent American justice.

$240 million had been paid by the end of 1998. Newspaper articles also indicated that the claims tribunals are likely to wind up their work this year.

Union Carbide's concern for the victims did not begin or end with the settlement it paid to them.

What Caused the Accident?

For days and weeks after the terrible chemical accident, rumors were running rampant about what had caused the deadly gas leak. Some people thought a fire had broken out, which resulted in several large explosions. This was even reported in the local media hours after the gas was first reported leaking. Other people thought that someone had accidentally mixed two or more chemicals together, which were supposed to be kept apart.

Rumors had always been circulating among some local residents about the quality of the workers that Union Carbide had been hiring to work with those dangerous chemicals. Some people felt that the employees who were hired were not properly trained and that they did not understand the magnitude and the danger of working around so many dangerous chemicals. In addition, some employees were not happy because they were not promoted, which led to job unrest and frequently a high turnover rate of employees.

Some employees later told investigators that cutbacks and layoffs had resulted in some procedures being changed. For example, they used to take readings and check MIC samples twice every shift, but eventually they cut back to only once a shift. To make matters worse, even the local Indian government had trouble keeping up with simple inspection procedures. The people whom the government had assigned to make inspections were mostly mechanical engineers, and those mechanical engineers had little or no knowledge of chemical engineering.

There was a local Indian pollution control board, but they had never even tested the Bhopal plant for any type of gas emissions. It was later discovered that even the local Indian air and water pollution control board failed to have the proper equipment necessary to measure air or water pollution.

Still other people thought that someone had deliberately caused the deadly gas leak. Little did those people realize at the time that they had guessed the true cause of the accident. In fact, it was established by Union Carbide and Indian investigators in March of 1985, after a 3-month special investigation, that a substantial amount of water had entered the tank. Investigators believed that the water had entered the MIC tank directly. Quoting from the Jackson Browning Report:

> Late in 1986, Union Carbide filed a lengthy court document in India detailing the findings of its scientific and legal investigations: the cause of the disaster was undeniably sabotage. The evidence showed that an employee of the Bhopal plant had deliberately introduced water into a MIC storage tank. The result was a cloud of poisonous gas. The episode is documented in a 17-minute videotape produced in 1988 by filmmaker Philip Gittelman, who was invited to undertake the documentary project by Union Carbide and its outside legal counsel. Kelley Drye and Warren of New York City. Also in 1988, an independent study of the incident by the prestigious international engineering consulting firm of Arthur D. Little supported the analysis by the Union Carbide team. Nothing the obstacles placed in the team's path by the

Indian Government, the Little Study said, "Had those constraints not been imposed, the actual cause of the incident would have been determined within several months." The Indian government, to this day, has not taken a firm position on the tragedy's cause, leaving Union Carbide's findings as the only definitive conclusion on the subject. The government of India has apparently decided not to pursue an investigation into the charge of employee sabotage.

A Later Look at Some Survivors

Within a year of the deadly chemical leak, the neighborhoods surrounding the Bhopal plant have been renovated. Visitors today would not recognize the area as being the same place. Gone are all traces of the gas leak, and people are trying hard to forget that terrible night and all of the tragedy that came with it.

Remember Sayed Abbas? The man who had awakened and found himself in the morgue after doctors accidentally declared him dead? He was but one of countless victims who would continue to suffer both physically and emotionally over the next few years. It seemed as if bad luck were following him long after that tragic night. After he ran from the morgue, Abbas was able to find his wife and two sons. His entire family continued to suffer from the effects of the deadly gas. When several black spots were discovered on Abbas's foot, the doctors mistakenly thought that gangrene had set in, and they amputated his leg. Unfortunately, it was not gangrene, but it was too late—his leg was gone. Shortly after the leg amputation, Abbas's youngest son died. Next, his mother became severely ill after she had returned to her village, and Abbas traveled there to be with her. She eventually did recover, and when Abbas returned to

his home his wife told him that their other son had also died.

Bitter by the whole experience and by the death of two of his sons, Abbas kept waiting for some type of settlement from the Indian government, but it was slow in coming. His simple repair business was starting to fail, and he was afraid he would go out of business before any help could arrive.

Remember Munnibai, the water woman at the train station? Her life was also changed forever by the tragic events of that December evening. She suffered from internal bleeding and could not open her eyes. Eventually, she was diagnosed with cancer, and doctors urged her to travel to Bombay to seek additional medical

Angry Bhopal residents seeking answers gather at the gate of Union Carbide plant one month after the chemical accident.

treatment. Munnibai refused, saying that she would rather not die someplace where her children were not nearby. A proud woman, she was deeply concerned for her family and returned to work to try and earn a meager living. No one had told her that victims of the gas leak that were too ill to return to work were eligible for a monetary settlement.

There are countless stories like those two, and even today people can tell you tales of someone they know who had been affected by the gas leak.

Despite the disaster that took place at that Union Carbide Bhopal plant in India, some positive changes have resulted. The tragedy brought awareness of chemical hazards and a new appreciation for environmental safety. Since December 3, 1984, many lives have been changed and many people have suffered, but people now have a better understanding of the dangers and risks involved when a plant is using hazardous materials.

Bibliography

Ashfaq, Ali. *Bhopal—Past and Present.* Bhopal: Jai Bharat Publishing House, 1981.

Chishti, Anees. *Dateline Bhopal: A Newsman's Diary of the Gas Disaster.* New Delhi: Concept Publishing Company, 1986.

Everest, Larry. *Behind the Poison Cloud.* Chicago: Banner Press, 1986.

Kurtzman, Dan. *A Killing Wind.* New York: McGraw-Hill, 1987.

Iyer, Pico. Clouds of uncertainty. *Time* December 24, 1984, pp. 24–27.

Morehouse, Ward, and Subramaniam, M. Arun. *The Bhopal Tragedy: What Really Happened and What It Means for American Workers and Communities at Risk.* New York: Council on International and Public Affairs, 1986.

Websites
www.bhopal.com

Further Reading

Bordewich, Fergus M. The lessons of Bhopal. *The Atlantic Monthly* March 1987, pp. 30–33.

Everest, Larry. *Behind the Poison Cloud.* Chicago: Banner Press, 1986.

Jones, Tara. *Corporate Killings: Bhopal Will Happen.* London: Free Association Books, 1988.

Kurtzman, Dan. *A Killing Wind.* New York: McGraw-Hill, 1987.

Weir, David. *The Bhopal Syndrome.* San Francisco: Sierra Club Books, 1987.

Index

Index

Index

Picture Credits

JOHN RIDDLE is a freelance writer and author from Bear, Delaware. His byline has appeared in major newspapers and magazines, including *The Washington Post* and *Curriculum Administrator*. He has also written for numerous websites, newsletters, and trade journals. He is the author of 17 books, including *The Story of the Pony Express, Steve Wozniak and the Story of Apple Computer,* and *Streetwise Guide to Business Management*. He is a frequent speaker at writers' conferences throughout the United States. More information about the author can be found on his website, *http://www.ilovetowrite.com*

JILL McCAFFREY has served for four years as national chairman of the Armed Forces Emergency Services of the American Red Cross. Ms. McCaffrey also serves on the board of directors for Knollwood—the Army Distaff Hall. The former Jill Ann Faulkner, a Massachusetts native, is the wife of Barry R. McCaffrey, who served in President Bill Clinton's cabinet as director of the White House Office of National Drug Control Policy. The McCaffreys are the parents of three grown children: Sean, a major in the U.S. Army; Tara, an intensive care nurse and captain in the National Guard; and Amy, a seventh grade teacher. The McCaffreys also have two grandchildren, Michael and Jack.